8|21

Get Crafting for Your
HIP HAMSTER

by Ruth Owen

BEARPORT
PUBLISHING

Minneapolis, Minnesota

CREATE!

Credits

Cover, © Olena Kurashova/Shutterstock and © Ruby Tuesday Books; 1, © Kingarion/Shutterstock and © Ruby Tuesday Books; 3, © Shutterstock; 4T, © Ruby Tuesday Books and © JazzBoo/Shutterstock; 4C, © Viachaslau Kraskouski/Shutterstock and © Ruby Tuesday Books; 4B, © Ruby Tuesday Books and © Timolina/Shutterstock; 5T, © Ruby Tuesday Books and © Kingarion/Shutterstock; 6, © Ruby Tuesday Books and © JazzBoo/Shutterstock; 7, © Ruby Tuesday Books; 8, © Ruby Tuesday Books; 9, © Ruby Tuesday Books; 10, © Ruby Tuesday Books; 11T, © Ruby Tuesday Books; 11B, © Ruby Tuesday Books and © irin-k/Shutterstock; 12L, © Ruby Tuesday Books; 12R, © stock_shot/Shutterstock; 13, © Ruby Tuesday Books; 14, © Ruby Tuesday Books and © areallart/Shutterstock; 15, © Ruby Tuesday Books; 16, © Ruby Tuesday Books; 17T, © Ruby Tuesday Books; 17B, © Ruby Tuesday Books and © Timolina/Shutterstock; 18, © Ruby Tuesday Books and © Kingarion/Shutterstock; 19, © Ruby Tuesday Books; 20, © Ruby Tuesday Books; 21T, © Ruby Tuesday Books; 21B, © Ruby Tuesday Books and © Olesya Zhuk/Shutterstock; 22TL, © Punyaphat Larpsomboon/Shutterstock; 22BL, © Punyaphat Larpsomboon/Shutterstock; 22R, © Tanyakim/Shutterstock; 23, © Vladimir Muravin/Shutterstock.

Library of Congress Cataloging-in-Publication Data

Names: Owen, Ruth, 1967- author.
Title: Get crafting for your hip hamster / Ruth Owen.
Description: Create! books edition. | Minneapolis, Minnesota : Bearport Publishing Company, [2021] | Series: Playful pet projects | Includes bibliographical references and index.
Identifiers: LCCN 2020042138 (print) | LCCN 2020042139 (ebook) | ISBN 9781647476632 (library binding) | ISBN 9781647476700 (ebook)
Subjects: LCSH: Hamsters as pets—Equipment and supplies—Juvenile literature. | Handicraft—Juvenile literature.
Classification: LCC SF459.H3 O94 2021 (print) | LCC SF459.H3 (ebook) | DDC 636.935/6—dc23
LC record available at https://lccn.loc.gov/2020042138
LC ebook record available at https://lccn.loc.gov/2020042139

For more information, write to Bearport Publishing, 5357 Penn Avenue South, Minneapolis, MN 55419. Printed in the United States of America.

CONTENTS

GET CRAFTY WITH YOUR HAMSTER

Are you the proud parent of a hamster, and do you love getting creative? If so, this is the perfect book for you! Discover four fantastic crafts that are fun to make and will give you and your hip hamster hours of enjoyment.

◀ Home Sweet Home
What could be more fun for your little pet than a carefully crafted hamster-sized playhouse?

Pet Snacks and Treats ▶
Always feed your hamster a healthy, **balanced diet**. But for a special treat, make your pet a homemade hamster cupcake!

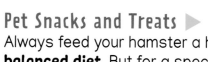

◀ Time to Play
Wild hamsters spend lots of time **foraging** for food. Scatter some food into this cardboard maze, and let your pet find its wild side!

Dress It Up ▶

Turn your little furry friend into a lovely ladybug by sewing this adorable snuggle pouch with a cozy fleece lining.

Have Fun and Be Safe

Crafting for your hip hamster can be lots of fun. But it's important that both you and your pet stay safe by following these top tips for careful crafting.

- Always get permission from an adult before making the projects in this book.

- Read the instructions carefully, and ask an adult for help if there's something you don't understand.

- Be careful when using scissors, and never let your hamster touch or play with them.

- Keep any glue where your pet can't sniff, lick, or touch it.

- When your project is complete, recycle any extra paper, cardboard, or packaging. Keep any leftover materials for a future project.

- Clean up when you've finished working.

- Remember! Some hamsters do well with gentle touching and attention. But others spend only a little time with their humans.

Never force your hamster to do something it seems unhappy to do.

HAPPY HAMSTER PLAYHOUSE

A hamster needs time to play and exercise outside of its cage. For hamster playtime, try making this delightful playhouse from popsicle sticks! Then, enjoy watching your furry friend explore.

If your hamster chews the playhouse, remove it from your pet's space.

You will need

- 112 popsicle sticks
- A ruler that is 1 inch (2.5 cm) wide
- A pencil
- Non-toxic glue
- An adult helper
- Scissors
- A piece of corrugated cardboard 6 in (15 cm) long and 1 in (2.5 cm) wide

1 To make the back wall of the house, lay 10 sticks side by side. Place the ruler so its top edge is even with the top edge of the sticks. Draw a pencil line along the ruler. Repeat on the bottom edge.

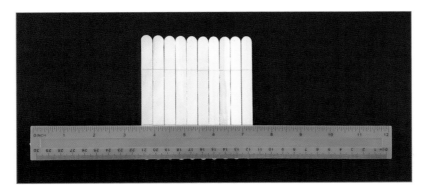

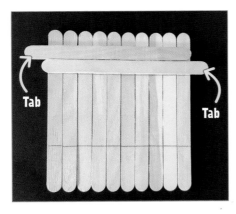

2 To join the sticks together, glue one stick directly above the top pencil line. Then, glue a second stick directly above the first and shifted over slightly.

> The ends of the sticks you've just glued will stick out to form tabs that you will need later for joining the four walls together.

3 Next, glue a stick directly below the bottom pencil line and glue a second stick below the first and shifted over slightly, as shown. Allow the glue to dry.

Finished back wall

4 To make a side wall, take 15 sticks and place them side by side. Using the ruler as a spacer, draw a pencil line at the top and bottom of the sticks, as you did in step 1.

5 Next, carefully move the last stick on each side away from the others to form a narrow gap. A popsicle stick placed on its edge should be able to easily slide into the gaps.

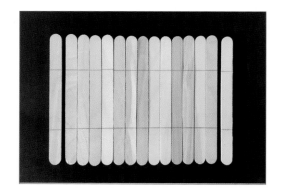

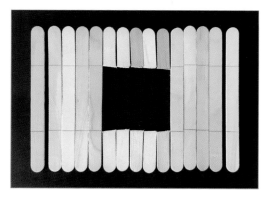

6 Glue on four sticks, positioning two above the top pencil line and two below the bottom pencil line. Be sure the sticks reach to the ends of the wall and overlap in the middle.

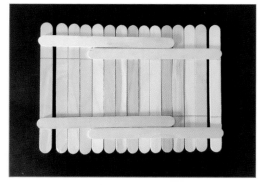

Inside of side wall

7 To make a side wall with a window, start by repeating steps 4 and 5. Then, take five sticks from the center and ask an adult helper to cut along the pencil marks on each stick. Place the top and bottom pieces of the cut sticks back in line.

8 Now, glue on four sticks just above the top pencil line and below the bottom line. Allow the glue to dry.

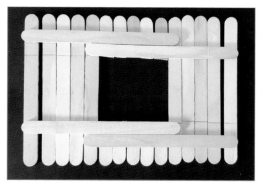

Inside of side wall with a window

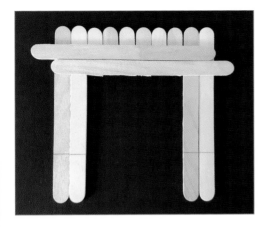

9 To make the front wall of the house, place 10 sticks side by side. Using the ruler as a spacer, draw a pencil line at the top and bottom of the sticks.

10 Take six sticks from the center and ask an adult helper to cut along the top pencil line. Place the smaller top piece of each stick back in line. Then, glue two sticks above the door, as shown.

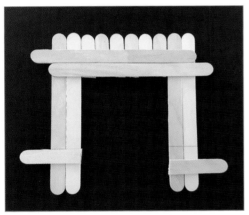

11 Ask your adult helper to use the leftover pieces of the sticks, and cut two short end pieces that are 1.5 in (3.8 cm) long. Glue these pieces below the bottom pencil lines, as shown. Allow the glue to dry.

Inside of front wall

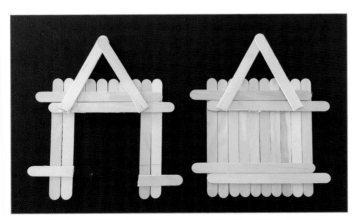

12 Next, ask your adult helper to cut four sticks 3 in (7.5 cm) long. Glue two of them to the inside of the front wall to make a triangle that will hold up the roof. Repeat on the back wall. Allow the glue to dry.

Inside of front wall   **Inside of back wall**

13 To assemble the house, slot two of the tabs from the back wall into the gap in one of the side walls, as shown.

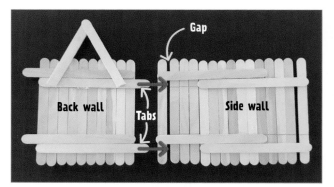

Gap

Back wall

Tabs

Side wall

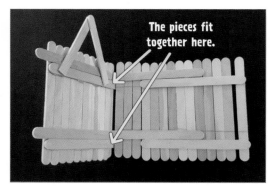

The pieces fit together here.

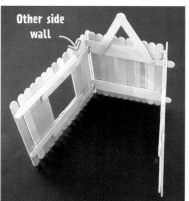

Other side wall

Front wall

14 Next, slide the two tabs on the other side of the back wall into the other side wall. Finally, take the front wall and slot its tabs into the empty ends of the side walls.

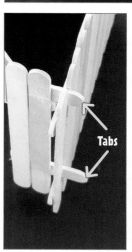

Tabs

15 To keep the tabs from moving, put glue on the front of the two tabs where the front wall meets a side wall. Then, take a stick and press it onto the glue-covered tabs. This stick will now lock the tabs in place. Repeat on the other three corners, and allow the glue to dry.

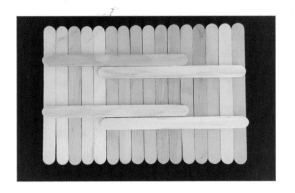

16 To make one side of the roof, take 16 sticks and lay them side by side. Glue four sticks across them. Repeat to make the other side of the roof. Allow the glue to dry.

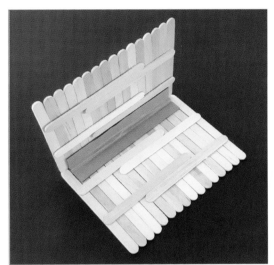

17 Take the piece of corrugated cardboard and fold it in half lengthwise. Glue one half of the cardboard to the inside edge of one roof piece. Allow to dry. Then, glue the other half of the cardboard to the other roof piece, as shown. Allow to dry.

The cardboard will create a hinge that holds the sides of the roof together.

18 Finally, set the roof on top of the two triangles. The playhouse is now ready for your hamster to move in!

A HIP HAMSTER HOUSE!

CRUNCHY CARROT CUPCAKES

In the wild, hamsters **hoard** food in their nests. They pack their cheek **pouches** so they can easily carry food home. Make your pet hamster this crunchy carrot cupcake. But don't be surprised if the treat quickly disappears into its bulging cheeks—it's just saving the goody for later!

You will need

- An adult helper
- A piece of peeled, washed carrot that's 1 in (2.5 cm) long
- A microwaveable bowl with a lid
- Water
- A small bowl
- 1/3 cup hamster seed mix
- 3 tablespoons all-purpose flour
- A spoon
- A baking sheet
- A fork

1 Ask your adult helper to preheat the oven to 300°F (150°C).

2 Put the carrot into the microwaveable bowl, cover the carrot with water, and then put on the lid loosely. Ask your adult helper to microwave the carrot for 5 minutes, or until it is soft. Then, ask them to drain the water. Leave it to cool.

Remember! These cupcakes should only be fed to your hamster as a treat.

3 Put the seed mix, 2 tablespoons of flour, and a tablespoon of water into a small bowl. Mix the ingredients until you have made a **dough**. Add a little more water if needed.

4 With your fingers, take a piece of dough about as big as a grape and mold it into a cupcake shape. Place the cupcake on the baking sheet. Keep making cupcakes until all the dough is used up.

5 To make the frosting, mash the soft carrot with a fork.

6 Add 1 tablespoon of flour to the mashed carrot and stir. Add water a little at a time if needed.

7 With your fingers, take a piece of frosting and press it onto the top of a cupcake. Repeat until all the cupcakes are frosted.

8 Ask your adult helper to bake the cupcakes for 15 minutes. Allow them to cool completely before giving one to your hamster.

MMM . . . SEED-A-LICIOUS!

MINI HAMSTER MAZE

Hamsters explore their world by moving their whiskers to feel around them. In fact, a hamster's whiskers can make about 30 tiny movements each second! Challenge your little explorer to find its way through this fun maze.

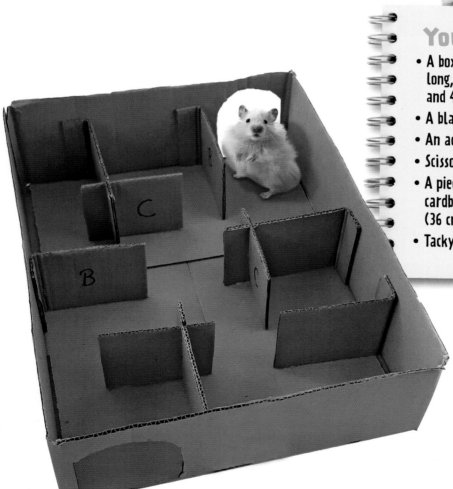

You will need

- A box that is 16 in (40.6 cm) long, 12 in (30.5 cm) wide, and 4 in (10 cm) high
- A black marker
- An adult helper
- Scissors
- A piece of corrugated cardboard that is a 14 in (36 cm) square
- Tacky glue

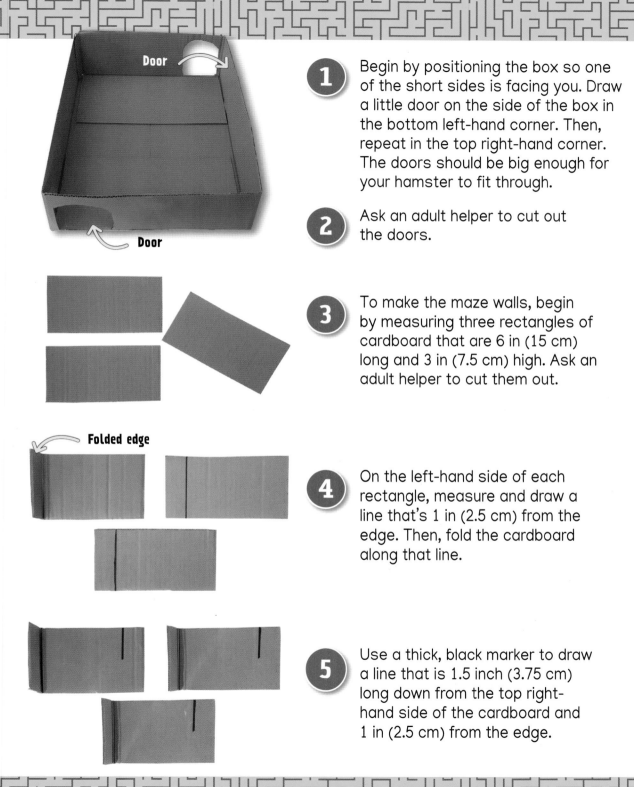

Door

Door

1 Begin by positioning the box so one of the short sides is facing you. Draw a little door on the side of the box in the bottom left-hand corner. Then, repeat in the top right-hand corner. The doors should be big enough for your hamster to fit through.

2 Ask an adult helper to cut out the doors.

3 To make the maze walls, begin by measuring three rectangles of cardboard that are 6 in (15 cm) long and 3 in (7.5 cm) high. Ask an adult helper to cut them out.

Folded edge

4 On the left-hand side of each rectangle, measure and draw a line that's 1 in (2.5 cm) from the edge. Then, fold the cardboard along that line.

5 Use a thick, black marker to draw a line that is 1.5 inch (3.75 cm) long down from the top right-hand side of the cardboard and 1 in (2.5 cm) from the edge.

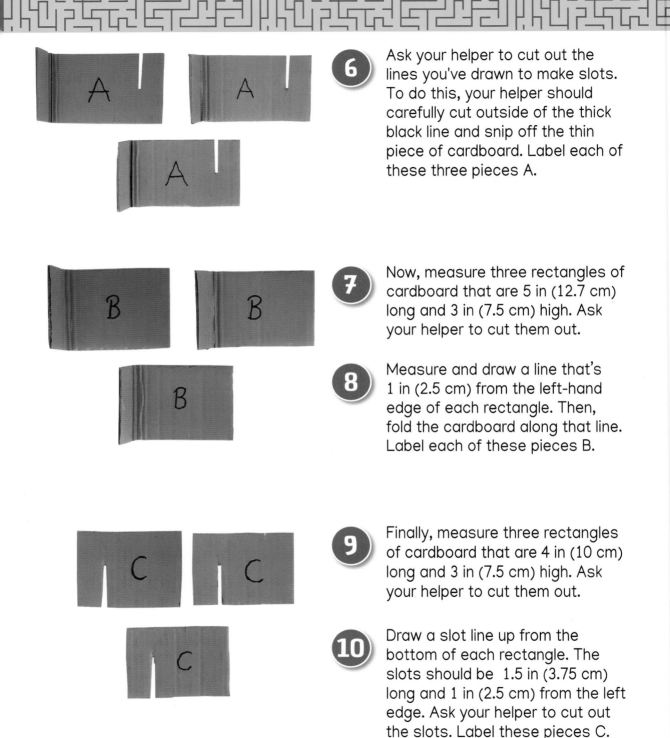

6 Ask your helper to cut out the lines you've drawn to make slots. To do this, your helper should carefully cut outside of the thick black line and snip off the thin piece of cardboard. Label each of these three pieces A.

7 Now, measure three rectangles of cardboard that are 5 in (12.7 cm) long and 3 in (7.5 cm) high. Ask your helper to cut them out.

8 Measure and draw a line that's 1 in (2.5 cm) from the left-hand edge of each rectangle. Then, fold the cardboard along that line. Label each of these pieces B.

9 Finally, measure three rectangles of cardboard that are 4 in (10 cm) long and 3 in (7.5 cm) high. Ask your helper to cut them out.

10 Draw a slot line up from the bottom of each rectangle. The slots should be 1.5 in (3.75 cm) long and 1 in (2.5 cm) from the left edge. Ask your helper to cut out the slots. Label these pieces C.

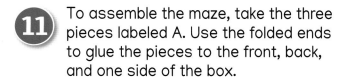

11 To assemble the maze, take the three pieces labeled A. Use the folded ends to glue the pieces to the front, back, and one side of the box.

12 Now, take the three rectangles labeled B. Glue them by their folded ends to the sides and back wall of the box.

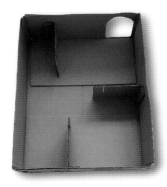

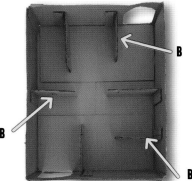

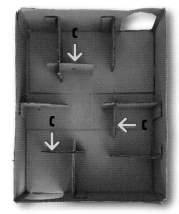

13 Finally, take the three rectangles labeled C. Match the slot of each piece C with the slot of a piece A, and slide piece C into place.

14 Put your hamster at one door of the maze and see if it can find its way to the other. Add some treats for your little pet to discover along the way!

LET'S GET SNIFFING AND EXPLORING!

SEW A SNUGGLE POUCH

This cute snuggle pouch can be placed in your hamster's cage as a cozy hideaway or a warm place to sleep. It can also be used to keep your little friend safe when you hold it on your lap or if you need to carry it around your home.

You will need

- A piece of soft fleece fabric and a piece of black fabric that are 12 in (30.5 cm) long and 6 in (15 cm) wide
- Sewing pins
- A needle
- Black thread
- A black marker
- Scissors
- A piece of red felt
- A piece of black felt
- White chalk
- A small bottle cap
- Tacky glue
- Red thread

Pin here

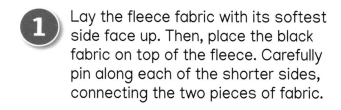

1 Lay the fleece fabric with its softest side face up. Then, place the black fabric on top of the fleece. Carefully pin along each of the shorter sides, connecting the two pieces of fabric.

2 Next, carefully sew along both lines of pins with black thread. Remove the pins and turn the two pieces of fabric inside out.

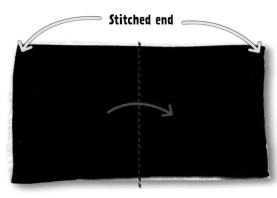

Stitched end

Always be careful when using pins. Be sure to keep the pins away from your hamster.

3 Lay the pouch flat with the black fabric on top. Then, fold the pouch in half so that the black fabric is sandwiched on the inside.

4 Drawing from the open end to the opposite end, use a marker to draw the shape of a ladybug's body onto the pouch. The open end should be the widest part of the ladybug's body. Then, pin along the lines, making sure to pin through all four layers of fabric.

5 Carefully sew along the two lines. Remove the pins.

6 Cut off the excess fabric corners to complete the shape of the bug's body. Then, turn the pouch inside out so the snuggly fleece is now on the inside.

7 To make the ladybug's wings, lay the pouch onto the red felt and trace around it with a marker. Cut out the shape.

8 Cut off a 1 in (2.5 cm) strip from the top edge of the wing piece. This strip is not needed. Then, cut the remaining large wing piece in half to make two sections.

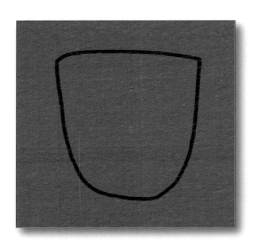

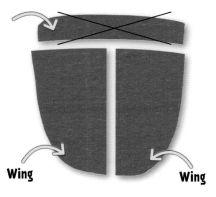

This piece is not needed.

Wing

Wing

9 To make spots for the wings, trace around the bottle cap with chalk onto the black felt. Repeat five more times to make six spots. Carefully cut out the spots.

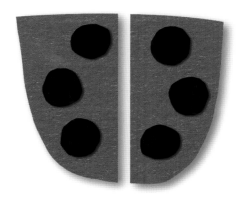

10 Glue three spots to each wing piece. Allow the glue to dry.

11 Finally, pin the top edge of each wing about 1 in (2.5 cm) from the open edge of the pouch. Be sure to pin through only to the top layer of the pouch. Following the line of pins, sew on the wings using red thread. Remove the pins.

The snuggle pouch is complete!

A CUTE AND COZY HAMSTER-BUG!

TOP TIPS FOR A HEALTHY, HAPPY HAMSTER!

Being a **responsible** hamster owner is all about keeping your pet healthy. Here are 10 tips to help you take care of your hip hamster.

1 Always get your hamster the biggest cage you can so it has lots of space for exercising.

2 Hamsters dig! Make sure your pet's cage has a thick layer of **bedding** that it can **burrow** into.

3 When you clean your hamster's cage, put back a small amount of dirty bedding so the cage still smells like home to your pet.

4 Keep your hamster away from TVs and computers. The sounds they make can be **stressful** to your pet.

5 Hamsters are **nocturnal**, which means they are active at night. Do not disturb them during the day when they are sleeping.

6 Refill your hamster's water bottle with fresh water each day.

7 Get to know how much your hamster eats each day. If it starts to eat less, take it to the vet right away.

8 To make feeding time more interesting, put some of your hamster's food in a small cardboard box for it to search out.

9 Your hamster should spend time out of its cage, but never leave it on its own.

10 Hamsters normally live for about two years. Only become a hamster parent if you are prepared to care for your pet for this whole time.

GLOSSARY

balanced diet eating foods in the correct amounts that contain everything needed for energy, health, and growth

bedding soft materials used to make a place for sleeping

burrow to dig down into soil or another material

dough a sticky, thick mixture of flour, water, and other ingredients that is used to make cookies, cakes, and breads

foraging looking for food in the wild

hoard to gather and hide away food or other objects

nocturnal active only at night

pouches pocket-like parts of an animal's body

responsible caring, trustworthy, and in charge

stressful making an animal or person feel anxious or afraid

INDEX

READ MORE

Brainard, Jason. *Is a Hamster a Good Pet for Me? (The Best Pet for Me)*. New York: PowerKids Press, 2020.

Colson, Mary. *The Truth About Hamsters: What Hamsters Do When You're Not Looking (Pets Undercover!)*. Chicago: Capstone, 2017.

LEARN MORE ONLINE

1. Go to **www.factsurfer.com**

2. Enter "**Crafting Hamster**" into the search box.

3. Click on the cover of this book to see a list of websites.

ABOUT THE AUTHOR

Ruth Owen has been developing and writing children's books for more than 10 years. She lives in Cornwall, England, just minutes from the ocean. Ruth loves all animals—wild and pets. Her favorite fact about hamsters is that they can stuff their cheek pouches with lots and lots of food!